DESERTS

AN ARID WILDERNESS

17987

JENNY WOOD

Gareth Stevens Children's Books
MILWAUKEE

Wonderworks of Nature:

Caves: An Underground Wonderland
Coral Reefs: Hidden Colonies of the Sea
Deserts: An Arid Wilderness
Icebergs: Titans of the Oceans
Rain Forests: Lush Tropical Paradise
Storms: Nature's Fury
Volcanoes: Fire from Below
Waterfalls: Nature's Thundering Splendor

For a free color catalog describing Gareth Stevens' list of high-quality children's books, call 1-800-341-3569 (USA) or 1-800-461-9120 (Canada).

Picture Credits:
Ardea — 10, 17, 20; Bruce Coleman — back cover, 5, 16, 18 (both), 22 (bottom); Robert Harding — 14 (bottom), 23; Hutchison — 19; Frank Lane — 6-7, 8 (top); Oxford Scientific Films — 12-13; Planet Earth Pictures — 9; Tony Stone — front cover; Survival Anglia — 8 (bottom), 14 (top), 15; Sygma — 22 (top); Zefa — 10-11

Illustration Credits:
All illustrations by Francis Mosley except pp. 24-28, Jon Davis/Linden Artists
Line art: Keith Ward

Library of Congress Cataloging-in-Publication Data

Wood, Jenny.
    Deserts : an arid wilderness / Jenny Wood.
        p. cm. — (Wonderworks of nature)
    Includes index.
    Summary: Explains the different types of deserts and how they are formed, as well as describing the first expedition to cross the desert of the Empty Quarter in Saudi Arabia.
    ISBN 0-8368-0631-X
    1. Deserts—Juvenile literature. [1. Deserts.] I. Title. II. Series: Wood, Jenny. Wonderworks of nature.
GB612.W66 1991
508.315'4—dc20   91-15814

This North American edition first published in 1991 by
Gareth Stevens Children's Books
1555 North RiverCenter Drive, Suite 201
Milwaukee, Wisconsin 53212, USA

This U.S. edition copyright © 1991. First published in the United Kingdom by Two-Can Publishing, Ltd. Text copyright © 1991 by Jenny Wood.

Printed in the United States of America

  2 3 4 5 6 7 8 9 97 96 95 94 93

CONTENTS

All words in **boldface** can be found in the glossary.

WHAT ARE DESERTS?

If you were asked to describe a desert, you would probably think of these three words: *hot, dry,* and *sandy*. But it is not as simple as that. Most of the world's deserts are in warm regions, but others, such as the Gobi Desert in Asia, can be extremely cold. In winter, temperatures there can reach as low as -40°F (-40°C). The areas around the North and South poles are classed as deserts, too, and they are extremely cold.

All deserts are dry. They receive less than 10 inches (25 cm) of rain or snow each year. But desert landscapes include gravel, boulders, and mountains. Sand covers only about 10 percent of most desert areas.

▶ Sand dunes in the Namib Desert of southwestern Africa.

▼ The world's main deserts. Although many scientists use the amount of annual rainfall to classify an area as a desert, some classify a desert by the type of soil and **vegetation**.

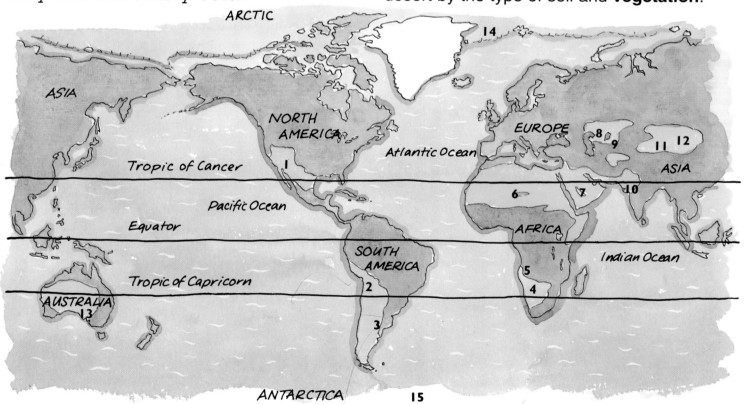

1 Great Basin (Death Valley, Mojave, Sonora, and Chihuahua deserts)
2 Atacama Desert
3 Patagonian Desert
4 Kalahari Desert
5 Namib Desert
6 Sahara Desert
7 Arabian Desert
8 Kara Kum
9 Kyzyl Kum
10 Thar Desert
11 Taklimakan Desert
12 Gobi Desert
13 Australian desert
14 North Pole
15 South Pole

HOW DESERTS ARE FORMED

Most deserts lie on either side of the equator, in areas known as the tropics. As warm air flows from the equator toward the tropics, it rises and cools. As the air cools, it releases its moisture as rain. By the time it reaches the tropics, the air is beginning to move down toward the land and warm up again. This warm air soaks up all the moisture in the ground below, and a dry desert area is created. The Sahara in Africa is a tropical desert.

Some deserts, such as the Taklimakan Desert in China, lie in

DID YOU KNOW?

● The only regular supply of moisture to the Namib Desert is the fog that rolls in from the cold southern Atlantic Ocean every day. Some creatures have developed ways of using this moisture. One beetle stands with its back to the incoming fog and allows moisture to condense on its body, then catches the water droplets as they trickle down its wings and into its mouth.

The formation of a rain-shadow desert

As air rises over the mountains, it cools and releases rain

Heavy rainfall

Warm air blows inland

Dry desert area

areas that are separated from the sea by mountains. Here, a type of desert known as a rain-shadow desert is created.

Coastal deserts, such as the Namib Desert in southwestern Africa, lie near the sea. Air masses move across the cold ocean waters and lose their moisture before reaching land.

Other deserts, such as the Gobi Desert and the Gibson Desert, are found in places far inland where the air is hot and dry.

◀ When rain falls in a desert, it usually comes as a sudden downpour. Water may collect in channels or dry lake beds.

SAND, ROCK, AND SALT

The appearance of deserts varies a great deal. High mountains, shifting sand dunes, vast expanses of stony ground, and huge boulders are all found in different deserts throughout the world. Some deserts include all these different types of landscapes. Desert areas like Death Valley in California have dried-up lake beds that are covered with a layer of glistening salt. Areas such as Antarctica are completely covered by a thick sheet of ice.

▲ If flood waters pouring down from surrounding hills cannot flow away, they become trapped in the desert valley and form a lake. As the lake dries out, it leaves a layer of salt. The layers of salt build up until the whole area becomes a **salt pan**.

◀ Sometimes all sand is blown away from a desert area, leaving only bare rocks.

▶ The tallest of the rock formations in Monument Valley, Arizona, rise as high as 984 feet (300 m). The landscape has been worn away over thousands of years to form flat-topped hills known as **mesas** and columns of rock called **buttes**.

HOT DESERTS

The Sahara is the world's largest hot desert. It stretches across northern Africa from the Atlantic Ocean in the west to the Red Sea in the east. Altogether, the Sahara covers about 3,475,000 square miles (9 million sq km).

During the last Ice Age, over ten thousand years ago, the Sahara had a much wetter climate, and the region was covered with grasslands and forests. About six thousand years ago, the climate in Africa became drier, and the

▲ Dunes form as wind blows grains of sand against obstacles and the sand piles up.

Scattered throughout the Sahara are fertile areas known as **oases**. Oases form in places where underground water flows to the surface or where there is a permanent river. The Sahara has about 90 large oases, where people live in villages and grow crops. Oases are a welcome sight to desert travelers.

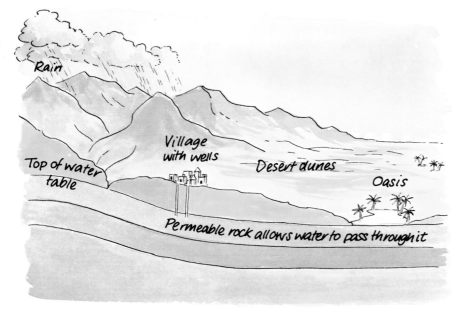

Rain

Top of water table

Village with wells

Desert dunes

Oasis

Permeable rock allows water to pass through it

Sahara slowly turned into a desert.

The Sahara is one of the hottest areas in the world. Temperatures as high as 136°F (58°C) have been recorded there. Large areas of the eastern and western Sahara receive less than 1 inch (2.5 cm) of rain each year.

The landscape of the Sahara is varied. The Ahaggar Mountains rise steeply in the center. A region of rocky **plateaus** known as the Tassili lies in the northeast. In the north and west of the Sahara are vast seas of sand called **ergs**.

▼ The fertile green area around an oasis is a strange desert sight.

DID YOU KNOW?

● Sand is actually tiny pieces of rock and **minerals** formed when larger rocks crumble away.

● Sand dunes keep moving. Strong winds can move a dune about 1 foot (30 cm) in a day. Some towns and settlements on the edge of a desert become gradually covered with sand, until people living there have to move.

● The toughest car race in the world is considered to be the Paris-Dakar Rally. The course starts in Paris, France, and crosses the Sahara Desert to end in Dakar, Senegal. The total distance is over 6,200 miles (10,000 km).

● Desert travelers sometimes see what they think is a pool of water in the distance. But when they reach the spot, they find only dry sand. The pool of water is an optical illusion known as a **mirage**. A mirage occurs when a ray of light ripples as it passes first through cold air and then through warm air.

COLD DESERTS

Cold deserts are found in the world's polar regions and on high mountains where the ground is frozen and there is little, if any, running water.

Antarctica is the coldest and iciest region in the world. A sheet of ice 7,200 feet (2,200 m) thick covers 98 percent of the continent. Much of the continent is a polar desert. Less than two inches (5 cm) of water falls every year, in the form of snow and ice crystals. The temperature rarely rises above 32°F (0°C) and has been known to drop as low as -128°F (-89°C).

You might think that nothing could live in this climate. But tiny plantlike organisms called algae grow on the ice and snow. Antarctica has no native human inhabitants, but about nine hundred scientists brave the Antarctic winters to operate

scientific stations there. Scientists study the ocean wildlife and the world's weather. The Arctic, on the other hand, is home to about two million people. Many Arctic lands have no snow and ice in summer, and Arctic inhabitants have found ways of adapting to the cold.

Both the Arctic and the Antarctic have rich stores of mineral deposits. Oil, gold, copper, and tin are mined in the Arctic. But in Antarctica, mining is forbidden for the time being. Many scientists worry that large-scale mining will harm Antarctica's **environment**.

KEEPING COOL

Animals that live in hot deserts have found ways of surviving in the hot, dry climate. Many are active at night, when temperatures are cool. During the day, they find shelter under rocks and plants, or in burrows. The animals that are

▼ Camels are well adapted for life in the desert. They can travel for days without having to eat or drink. The fat contained in a camel's hump provides the animal with the energy it needs.

▶ A sidewinder snake holds its head half-buried in the sand. Sidewinders move sideways across the sand, keeping most of their body above the ground.

◀ The Gila monster is a type of lizard found in the deserts of the United States and Mexico. It moves very slowly, but it has fangs like a snake's and can kill prey with its **venomous** bite. The Gila monster stores fat in its tail and can survive for months without food.

active in the daytime heat have ways of keeping their bodies away from the burning sand. The Saharan jerboa and the American kangaroo rat, for example, have long back legs that allow them to hop quickly over the ground. The frilled lizard of the Australian desert also runs quickly on its back legs.

Creatures such as snakes and lizards, which are cold-blooded, need to warm themselves in the heat of the sun before they can move around. They hide in the shade when the sun is at its hottest.

The main problem for desert animals is the lack of water. Some have found ways of storing water in their bodies. Others get all the moisture they need from the plants and insects they eat.

Like many desert animals, the fennec of the Sahara has large ears. These help the animal lose heat from its body and stay cool.

THE FLOWERING DESERT

Like desert animals, desert plants have also developed ways of using every available drop of water. Some have long, tough roots that burrow deep underground in search of moisture. The roots of mesquite bushes in the deserts of the southwestern United States can burrow as deep as 39 feet (12 m).

Many cacti have roots that spread over a wide area just below the ground's surface. Water travels up through the roots into the stem of the plant, which can store water.

Plants lose water through their leaves, so in dry desert areas many plants have tiny leaves that allow only a small amount of water to escape. Others shed their leaves during long, dry periods.

A number of plants do not grow at all during periods of **drought**. They lie as seeds in the soil, waiting for rain. When rain falls, the seeds **germinate** very quickly and, within a few days, the desert is a mass of color.

DID YOU KNOW?

● Cacti can live as long as 200 years.

● The leaves of the desert holly grow almost vertically. This means that the fierce heat of the sun catches only the edges of the leaves, and so they lose very little moisture.

● As much as 80 percent of a giant saguaro cactus may be water.

● The stems of the jumping cactus plant break off very easily and seem to jump onto any person or animal that passes by. The spines can cause painful wounds.

▶ The saguaro cactus stores water in its stem. After rain has fallen, cacti swell as they fill up with water. They live on this stored water until the next rains come. Saguaros, found in North American deserts, may reach a height of 60 feet (18 m). In spring, flowers bloom on the tips of their branches and stems.

▼ The Kalahari Desert in bloom after a rare period of rain. The flowers bloom for only a few days until the desert dries out again.

WIND, WATER, AND HEAT

Although very little rain falls in desert areas, much of the shaping of the desert landscape is caused by water. When rain does fall, it is very heavy. The hard, dry soil cannot soak up the water, so it runs down slopes, causing **flash floods**. The water carves out steep-sided valleys known as **wadis**. Rocks, boulders, and pebbles are carried

▶ This incredible boulder was created by wind and water **erosion**.

down from the valleys onto the desert plain.

Wind also helps sculpture desert areas. Sand dunes are formed by wind, but sometimes the sand and soil are blown away completely, leaving bare rock surfaces known as rock pavements. Wind blows the sand with such force that any large rocks in its path are eroded.

Rocks on the surface of a desert are affected by heat, too. During the day, they are heated. At night, the rocks cool down. This constant heating and cooling weakens the rocks until eventually they crack.

▲ Eroded sandstone columns stand tall in the Tassili plateaus of the Sahara.

◀ These badlands lie on the Arizona-Utah border. Badlands are barren areas of small, steep hills and deep valleys that have been worn away by wind and water.

Wadis are created by water rushing down desert slopes. They are dry for most of the year.

Flash floods rush downhill

Loose rocks, boulders and pebbles

Wadi

SURVIVING IN THE DESERT

The way of life for many desert peoples has changed in recent years. Many, such as the Bedouins of the Middle East and northern Africa, used to be **nomads**. They had no permanent homes but put up temporary shelters wherever they stopped. They lived by trading with other desert peoples, exchanging goods such as wool and leather for rice and grain. Their animals provided meat and milk as well as wool and skin for clothing and tents.

Although a few nomadic tribes still follow this traditional way of life, most have abandoned it.

Some still spend part of each year traveling, but others now live in permanent campsites or oasis villages where they can grow crops. Still others have moved to towns and cities in search of work.

One reason for these changing ways is that governments have made it more difficult for people to travel freely among countries. Also, severe droughts have made it even more difficult for people and animals in these areas to survive.

▼ Many Kurds, who live in an area of high mountains in Asia known as Kurdistan, are nomads. They live in tents and are skilled in breeding cattle, horses, sheep, and goats.

COLLECTING WATER

A desert traveler will often make a **solar still** in order to collect water to drink. In hot weather, try making your own to see how one works. A beach or a sandbox would be a good place to do this.

You will need:
- A shovel
- A jar or tin can
- A sheet of plastic wrap
- Stones

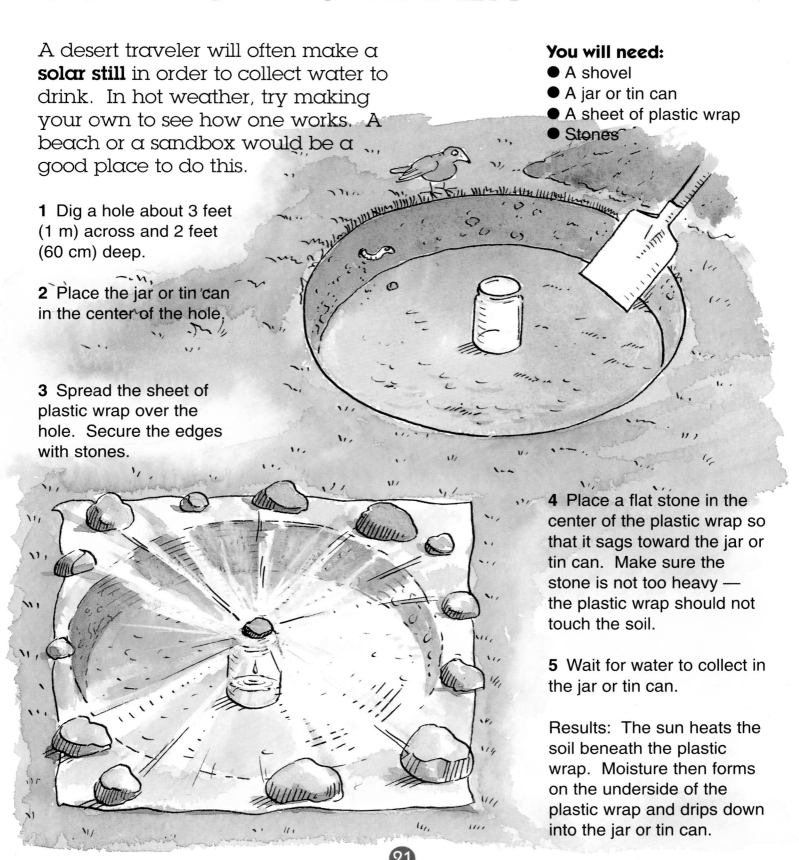

1 Dig a hole about 3 feet (1 m) across and 2 feet (60 cm) deep.

2 Place the jar or tin can in the center of the hole.

3 Spread the sheet of plastic wrap over the hole. Secure the edges with stones.

4 Place a flat stone in the center of the plastic wrap so that it sags toward the jar or tin can. Make sure the stone is not too heavy — the plastic wrap should not touch the soil.

5 Wait for water to collect in the jar or tin can.

Results: The sun heats the soil beneath the plastic wrap. Moisture then forms on the underside of the plastic wrap and drips down into the jar or tin can.

SCIENCE AT WORK

Desert lands are so dry that growing crops is difficult. Scientists have developed ways of watering the ground in some desert areas to make it fertile. Where there is water on the surface, a network of canals is built to carry water from the lake or river to the farmlands. Where water lies underground, wells are dug to pump the water to the surface. Watering desert lands in this way is known as **irrigation**.

Desert lands contain some of the world's most valuable mineral deposits. Diamonds are now mined in the Namib Desert in southwestern Africa, and there are huge copper and **sodium nitrate** mines in the Atacama Desert in South America. Gold, uranium,

▲ Each of these circular wheat fields in Libya is watered by a long pipe on rails that rotates like the hands of a clock. Water is pumped from underground.

◄ Narrow ditches called furrows carry water between rows of crops. The water flows through a pipe and pours out through openings in the pipe into the furrows.

and aluminum have been discovered in the Australian desert, and large quantities of oil and natural gas lie beneath the Sahara, Arabian, and American deserts.

Deserts receive huge amounts of light and heat from the sun. Some of the sunlight in desert areas can now be captured and turned into **solar energy**. Hundreds of flat or slightly curved mirrors are laid out over an area of desert land. The mirrors focus the sun's rays onto a target. A fluid is pumped through the target and heated. As the fluid warms, it produces steam or some other vapor, which then carries heat energy to turbines that generate electricity in a nearby power station.

▲ An open-pit copper mine in Arizona. The copper-bearing rock is removed from horizontal layers called benches that run up and around the sides of the pit.

DID YOU KNOW?

● Deserts are on the move. Each year, many of the world's deserts increase in size. One of the main reasons for this is that fertile land along the edges of the deserts is being made barren by cattle and other livestock stripping the ground bare of all its vegetation. Huge mining projects, as well as the destruction of trees, also have a part to play in this process, known as *desertification*.

THE SEARCH FOR THE LOST CITY

British explorer Harry Philby could not remember when he had first heard the name "Wabar." But as soon as he heard the legend, he decided to be the one to find the lost city. Storytellers told of the fabulous capital of King Ad Ibn Kin'ad that lay buried deep in the Rub' al Khali Desert in Arabia, with palaces encrusted with gems and surrounded by gardens bright with exotic flowers. Here, the king's glittering court had feasted and played until at last the wrath of God had descended upon them, destroying the city with fire.

The city of Wabar had been lost for seven thousand years. The river on whose banks it was supposed to have lain had long since vanished, covered over by the shifting desert sands. The desert was known to the Arabs as "the Empty Quarter." The Arabs warned of the terrible dangers that lay within it. The sands, they said, were littered with the bleached skeletons of travelers

the campfire talking, he fainted. His face turned yellow and his companions were convinced that he was going to die. They covered him with blankets to keep him warm and took turns watching over him until morning. When Philby awoke, he felt perfectly fine. The mysterious illness had passed.

The expedition moved on. It seemed cursed with bad luck all the way. First the weather turned bitterly cold, so cold that the drinking water froze in the skins the men carried. Then, a few days later, it became unbearably hot. The line of camels trudged on through the sand. Grains of sand were whipped up all around the members of the party, turning their faces raw and getting into every crevice of their clothing.

and their camels who had perished in the burning heat.

But Philby was determined. On January 6, 1932, he set out with eighteen men and thirty-two camels loaded with supplies. On the first night, as Philby stood by

Soon their water ran out. The men spent much of the day searching for wells buried deep in the sand. When they found the wells, they had to spend hours digging before the water could be reached.

The party crossed the beds of two ancient, dried-up rivers and eventually came to a third. Philby believed this was the river beside which the city of Wabar had once stood. At last they camped within a day's journey of Wabar. Philby tossed and turned in bed that night, haunted by dreams of the long-dead city.

The next day the men continued their march, following the river's dusty course.

"Look!" shouted one of the party's guides suddenly.

Philby shaded his eyes against the glare of the sun. On the crest

of a distant ridge, he saw what appeared to be a thin, low line of ancient ruins.

He urged his camel on, thrilled by the prospect of making his dream into reality. It took many hours to reach the top of the ridge,

and the sky was darkening as Philby jumped down from his camel and ran across the sand to the wall.

He sank to his knees with a groan. He was looking down at the remains of two meteorite explosions encircled with low walls of rock and half-filled with drifting sand. Harry Philby realized with overwhelming disappointment that the centuries-old legend still lay hidden beneath the shifting sands of the Rub' al Khali Desert.

His guides demanded that the expedition leave. But Philby wanted to accomplish something on the trip and ordered them to keep moving across 360 miles (580 km) of burning, waterless desert.

The men pressed on into the drought-stricken land. The rocks and sand seemed to vibrate with the heat, and the camels became exhausted. The food and water had almost been used up. On March 14, they finally emerged from the desert, the first people in history to cross the Empty Quarter from east to west.

TRUE OR FALSE?

**Which of the statements below are true and which are false?
If you have read this book carefully, you will know the answers.**

1 Sand consists of tiny pieces of rock and minerals.

2 All deserts are hot.

3 Most desert animals are active during the day.

4 The Sahara used to be covered with grasslands and forests.

9 The temperature in a hot desert falls dramatically at night.

10 Rain-shadow deserts lie on coasts.

11 Many desert peoples no longer follow a nomadic way of life.

5 Mesas and buttes are types of cacti.

6 Oases are fertile areas in a desert.

7 Sand covers half of all desert areas.

8 A mirage is an optical illusion.

12 Some desert plants store water in their stems.

GLOSSARY

Buttes are columns of rock in desert areas where the surrounding stone has been worn away by wind, water, and heat.

Drought is a long period of dry weather with little or no rainfall at all.

Environment is a word used to describe a region that includes everything that affects it, including its landscape, its human, animal, and plant life, and its weather.

Ergs are huge areas of sand in the Sahara Desert.

Erosion is the gradual wearing away of the earth's surface.

Flash floods are sudden, violent floods that occur when rain falls in a desert. Because the ground is so hard and dry, the water cannot soak in and so it rushes over the surface. The force of the water eventually wears away the land.

Germinate means to start growing and, in the case of plants, to produce new shoots.

Irrigation means building canals or digging wells to carry water to dry desert areas in order to make them suitable for growing crops.

Mesas are large, flat-topped hills. They are formed over thousands of years by the effects of wind, water, and heat wearing away the rock.

Minerals are natural substances like metals and ores that can be dug or mined from under the ground and used in different ways by humans.

Mirage is an optical illusion caused by heat. In the desert, a mirage often causes people to believe they see a pool of water in the distance.

Nomads are people who have no permanent home, but travel from place to place, building temporary shelters wherever they stop. Many nomads own herds of grazing animals like cattle, sheep, or goats.

Oases are fertile areas in a desert where underground water flows to the surface, or where there is a permanent river.

Plateaus are areas of high, level land.

Salt pans form when water dries out from a desert lake, leaving only a layer of salt.

Sodium nitrate is a type of crystallized salt that can be used to make matches, explosives, and fertilizers.

Solar energy is energy given off by or derived from the sun.

Solar still is a system of extracting water from the ground using the sun's heat.

Vegetation means the plant life of a particular area.

Venomous means poisonous.

Wadis are steep-sided valleys in desert areas that have been carved out by water.

INDEX